A Pocketful of Virtues, Book One
Kindness, Perseverance, Curiosity
And Patience

Written by Sharon Kuhn Young
Illustrated by Jordan Roberts

A Pocketful of Virtues, Book One

By Sharon Kuhn Young

Illustrated by Jordan Roberts

Ingram Spark Publishing

Copyright © 2020 Sharon Kuhn Young and Jordan Roberts

ISBN: 978-0-578-63405-0

To contact the author please email: pocketfulofvirtues@gmail.com

Foreword

Sharon Kuhn Young has been my friend and co-conspirator for the past 4 decades. I have read her work about life and children with delight, humor and the subtle grab at the heart. It is my pleasure to write this forward about this insightful new book series, A Pocketful of Virtues, that comes with the possibility of a huge impact on the lives of young children.

Believing that virtues help to form a child's character, Sharon provides ways to introduce and talk about these characteristics through age appropriate examples and illustrations. Virtues are often learned through imitation and habit; unfortunately not every child has a positive role model, family or otherwise. It is the author's hope to bring to light these virtues by way of mentors, teachers, educational institutions and community programs.

A Pocketful of Virtues is written without religious preference and is accessible and appropriate for groups of children from all races and cultures. A Pocketful of Virtues focuses on universal behaviors that will most probably have a positive impact on their lives and the lives of others.

Recognizing that virtues can be interpreted and taught in various ways, A Pocketful of Virtues is meant to provide a foundation for a thoughtful discussion, a Kickstarter, so to speak, with a trusted source so that the child can formulate her or his own ideals and behaviors.

A word of caution, as you begin this new series, your pockets will soon be filled with things you can share with children of all ages!

The Rev. Dr. Ellen Shepard
Assistant Professor in Practical Theology, Emory University
Pastor, Stone Mountain First United Methodist Church

Written in honor of my mother, Betty Kuhn Brouthers, who lived a life celebrating and sharing the small things that made a huge difference in the lives of so many.

Dedicated to my nieces and nephews David, Paul, Jonathan, Mark, Julia, Alicia and Kristen; the children I fell in love with and the amazing adults they have become. For them, their children and their children...

Always, Aunt Sharon (AKA Tia)

I have a secret pocket
That no one knows is there.
And in my secret pocket
I keep things I like to share.

Today I want to share with you
Some ways you can be kind,
After every act of kindness given
A smile is what you'll find.

Kiss your grandma on her cheek,
Share your favorite toy.
Smile at your neighbor,
Spread a little joy!

Hug your baby sister,
Teach your brother how to throw.
Give your dad a helping hand,
Use the manners that you know.

Be gentle with all animals,
Treat your pets the way you should.
Invite somebody out to play
Who is new to your neighborhood.

Pick somebody on your team
Who seems to need a friend.
And never be a bully
When you can be kind instead.

Be mindful of the things you say,
Be thoughtful in what you do,
Your acts of kindness will multiply
So others have a pocketful too!

Perseverance is a grown-up word
And this is what it means -
Never give up, keep on trying,
And always chase your dreams.

Finish your homework, start your project,
Study for your test.
Even when you'd rather play,
Persevere and do your best!

If you're practicing an instrument
Or learning how to spell,
You'll get better every day you say,
"I can do this, and do this well!"

Learn to swim, or ride a bike,
Climb a mountain, or run a race.
When you reach your goal at last,
You'll have a smile upon your face.

There will be days when you have problems,
Don't quit, don't stop, be strong!
Your pocketful of perseverance
Will last your whole life long.

When you reach the place you're going
You will hold a prize so dear,
A job well done, a challenge won
Because you persevered.

Curiosity

Curiosity makes you question
The how's and who's and why's,
And like an explorer you'll set sail
For the journey in your mind.

Why are clouds so fluffy and white?
Why is the sky so blue?
Who invented bubble gum?
All these things you never knew!

Why are giraffes so very tall?
How do birds learn how to fly?
How come zebras have their stripes?
We've always wondered why.

Are oceans bigger than the sky?
How far away are the stars?
How does the rain make rainbows?
Will we ever live on Mars?

The questions that you ask
And the answers you discover,
Fill your pocket full of knowledge-
That makes you like no other!

When you wonder about things around you,
When curiosity fills your mind,
The world becomes your classroom -
Oh, the wonders you will find!

Patience

Patience is being able to accept
A bothersome event or delay.
It's not losing your temper or being grumpy
When something upsets your day.

Patience is sometimes hard to find
But you'll never run out once you know.
That the more you use it, the more you'll have -
Your patience like you will grow!

Think of all the times that someone
Has worked patiently with you.
When they taught you how to read and write
Or how to tie your shoe!

It's easy to be impatient
When we're waiting to have some fun,
Like a birthday party, or flying a kite,
Or a day at the beach in the sun!

Who should you be patient with?
Your friends, your mom, your dad,
Your brother and your sister,
Even when you're feeling mad.

Remember that patience never runs out.
So, when you start your day,
Take your pocketful of patience
And give all of it away!

Kindness and curiosity,
Perseverance and patience too,
Keep them in your pocket
To use with EVERYTHING you do!

Part of growing up is learning
What makes you YOU and what makes me ME.
You'll decide every day, what to do, what to say,
To become the best YOU, you can be.

Discussion Questions and Activities

Kindness

Give an example of something kind that a friend or family member has done for you.   How did it make you feel?

Can you think of an act of kindness you have done for someone? How do you think it made the other person feel? How did it make you feel?

What is an act of kindness that you could share with a member of your family this week?

What is something kind that you could do for a friend or someone you go to school with?

Is there someone you know of who could use more kindness from you and others? Who and Why? How can you show that person kindness?

Perseverance

Name something that is hard for you to finish. Like cleaning your room, a homework project, practicing a sport or practicing an instrument?

Think of a time when you felt tired or bored and did not want to finish something. Why should you finish things? Is being tired or bored a reason to stop? What could you do differently to get back to the task?

Who is someone you know that seems to always keep trying their best at whatever they are doing? Do you admire this person? If yes - why?

Have you finished something and felt really good about it? Tell us about that experience.

Name something you want to accomplish and talk about a plan to persevere to get it done.

Curiosity

Do you tend to ask questions when you are curious about something or someone?

Do you think asking questions helps you to learn? How and why?

When you have a question about something you have wondered about, who can you go to with your questions?

What are some other places you can go to do research and learn about things?

Let's make a list of these topics and then make a list of which adult(s) you can ask to help you find the answers.

Do you think you will continue to learn new things as you grow older?

Patience

Name a time when someone was patient with you or with someone you know. How did you know they were being patient?

How do you feel when you are patient with someone who needs your help?

Have you ever been very impatient for something to start?
Which kinds of events?

What did they mean when they said that the more you use patience, the more you will have? Is patience something you can practice?

Let's make a list of some things you can do to help you from becoming impatient?

In Closing

Which of the virtues kindness, perseverance, curiosity and patience is your favorite? Why?

Do you think that learning and practicing these virtues will help others?

CPSIA information can be obtained
at www.ICGtesting.com
Printed in the USA
LVHW020855230520
656349LV00025B/223